EARTH'S BLACK CHUTE

Earth's Black Chute

Cian Ferriter

SOUTHWORDeditions

First published in 2022
by Southword Editions
The Munster Literature Centre
Frank O'Connor House, 84 Douglas Street
Cork, Ireland

Set in Adobe Caslon 12pt

Copyright © 2022 Cian Ferriter

ISBN 978-1-905002-92-4

Contents

To Deirdre: up to the moon

CHUTE

No scratch of otter-claw on stone,
nor badger filling her sett with ancient heat.
No owl-heart pulsing on a ledge of ash.

So when, on this Atlantic headland,
stepping around tight arguments of gorse,
I stumble on a hare's still-warm body,

I kneel to press my ear to hers,
to the noises of the underworld:
murmurings and moanings taking flight,

loosening of entrails and fire,
stretch and snap of afterbirth,
animal breath dripping from cave roofs,

trapdoors swinging open, then shut.
Time's dark star collapsing into dusk,
I slip headlong down earth's black chute.

Garden Shed

Through the shed's squat door,
I am back to a tower block
in East Berlin before the fall

where every night at ten
the State-employed caretaker,
with the B-movie limp,

locked our flat door from the outside
and where, at midnight,
the man in the flat above

dropped empty beer bottles
onto the concrete plaza below,
glass exploding as he roared

expressions in old German
(consisting, we learned later, of a series
of agricultural curses

directed largely at his mother);
our door unlocked again at dawn
although by whom, we never saw.

SNOWBALL

I have fallen out of the world
this February night and landed here
at the marsh's edge, reeds about me
like the masts of listing galleons.

I can go no further. A newt
flexes his crested spine like the dragon
on the silk gown of the Emperor Zhu Di –
he of Perpetual Happiness –

as he watches what remains of his fleet
limp into the swollen mouth of the Yangtze,
mist rising, his eunuch entourage
readying for retreat to the hills;

his departure, later, marked by a single
gong of the North Temple's bell,
horse hooves disappearing into the wood,
the moon a snowball breaking on a black roof

and landing now six hundred years on
as droplets on my brow,
my pallor the Emperor's pallor
as he starts at a rustle in the undergrowth

and contemplates for the first time
the terror of death.

GHOST SHIP

I have seen your house adrift in the strangest
of places: in Cassidy's top field, smoke
spilling from the chimney. In a clearing
in Hartigan's Wood, wet shirts hanging
between two pines. Against the stump of the keep

beyond Moran's, the crooked gable-end
taking rain; and, one night, jutting out
over the lip of the quarry, a light on
in the kitchen, the whole place teetering –

This morning, in thinning mist, it is back
where you last left from it. Lace curtains
neatly parted, lavender turning to spit,
crab-apples pocking the grass. The gate-latch
rattling like a freshly-turned prayer wheel.

REPUBLIC

The River

The eddies, where she entered, scattered like eels,
her mother's fur coat in the downdraft
was a raft of otters turning for the deep.
The 9 bus on the bridge above crossed
from north to south, its driver nearing shift-end.

Her ripples were no bigger than a carp's,
her weight displaced in the dark flow,
the same weight I see in her daughter,
and in her daughter's daughter,
when we cast through midge-clouds in evening heat.

The Search

There were things the old hands took as signs,
starting the search at Lady's Island:
a curlews' nest empty in July –
a sword handle staking the mud at low tide,
its jade dragon spitting fire –
engraved, above the initials MMcE,
'Korea '50 to '53'.

They found her hat on an alder branch
hanging the way it hung in the hall.

The Funeral

The cortege stretched a good half mile,
a slow tributary bending the streets black
before sliding into the cemetery's basin.

No headstone yet over her husband's grave,
although the anniversary had long passed.

She couldn't bring herself to visit, it was said.
Flowers withered there like weeds sprayed in a ditch.

They came from as far as Derry,
her people in the main.
Men sweating in suits,
women touching mantillas.

Some of the talk was angry, all of it was low –
how does a mother do that to her own?

My Mother

I wheel my mother along the shore path,
because she's always loved the water.
Her hair blow-dried, white, shining in the sun,
pipits flitting and skipping in the shallows.

I recall the day on *Silver Strand* when she bolted,
naked, into the Atlantic, and we followed
her lead, roaring at the big sky,

our togs strung out along the sand
like a clothesline had been yanked
from its posts and thrown over the shoulder
of a mother proclaiming her own Republic.

The Sea

She points to where to stop. We stop.
She folds her hands, her eyes closing in the warm breeze.
My hands rest on her sparrow shoulders,

our pulses merging,
the sea taking all the river has to give.

Last Rites

Uncle Jack once gripped a man's half-severed hands
while giving him last rites in Santiago.
Bullets puffing dirt from broken ground,
clothes strung above them in the narrow street
like echoes of the dead or missing.

He gave up speech at last, sought answers
in what leaked through night-time's cracks.
Bare bulb flickering in his top-floor flat.
Dawn-light catching the sides of ashtrays,
cats tip-toeing between bottles.

A man who put others before himself
who fell holding out his hands to rain,
to his shadow opening large to meet him,
to love on the other side, waiting,
to clay returning, without interest, to clay.

My Uncle the Recluse

Not in the guidebooks, that ruin; no signs
or gravelled path. My father and the others
in the roofless rectangle where the monks
once vespered. Candled sycamores, crusted
cowpats, yellowing grass, the usual.

I had wandered around the back, naming off
the breeds – *Hereford, Charolais, Kerry Blue* –
when the bull made for me, all haunch
and shuddering neck, too big and gleamy
for himself. I tried to roar but no sound emerged

until two hands like warm stones fixed
my shoulders. *Stand your ground! He'll not
breach that fence.* My uncle. A row of flowering
thistles between us and the barbed wire's
spikes and – I'm sure of it – steam

rising from the bull's nostrils, his ring
a chieftain's torc. Shouts from the abbey.
Jackdaws swooping from a copse. And later,
the whole journey back, my uncle tight beside me
staring out at small fields, scattering rooks.

Keeper

Sure I'd best do it myself
the words from your silhouette
at the front door at Crewbawn,
morning light settling around you,
the Boyne beyond, bending the earth.

By the time I follow you out,
arms puckered with stings,
you are high up the alder tree,
head lost in a swarm
of bees like a man leaning in

through a hatch. Thunderclap
as your box slaps closed,
left neat by the front step
as you recede into the yard.

Later, your dusty red Datsun
pushing off down the avenue,
bees flooding the back window
like coins pouring into a hold.

The Others

It was our scary film phase –
Friday nights in the living room,
biscuits, milky tea –
before I drifted out into adulthood.

I remember the start you got
– nail-marks on my arm, *Jesus Christ!* –
at the end of that scene
where a young girl is playing alone

in a room in a Gothic mansion,
singing to herself, back to the viewer,
and then turns suddenly, her face
an 80-year old's, long dead.

When I came to visit recently,
I was the one to start when you turned
with a child's mild devastation
before returning wordlessly to the screen,

your white hair sticking out
over the top of the armchair
like a stand-in dummy
among discarded props.

End Place

I am leaning over a bridge
when my grandmother floats past,
her white face kissing lilies.

Upstream, a fisherman
is lost in Gulliver's boots,
his rod arguing with the universe.

No sign of her on the other side.
Insects mote the air.
In the reeds, a heron's shadow.

Between deciduous trees,
pockets of kidnapped light
list in mud.

My ears fill with water's noise –
rinsed stone and pebble,
loosened cries.

The river tumbles onwards
to its end-place, heron-wings
filling the slant sky.

SILAGE

from the jeep window
in the jungle's airless choke

ampersands
of swinging monkeys

leeches stippling the belly
of a wounded hog

a man kneeling blindfolded
in a clearing

shot of a back-firing
exhaust

an inked woman
bent under a basket

a bell ringing
in an abandoned temple

puddles in rutted muck
reflecting the sky

your face
seeping through

from a puddle in a yard
half the world away

you pitching silage
cattle heads straining through bars

in the place
you never left from

and I can't get away from still

Last Tour

(Hardware store, Missouri, mid-July)

The Discount for Vets sign brings him in,
the house badly in need of fixing.

Stars and stripes limp on high poles in the lot.
Rounding the aisle, paint-pots crash –

now he's back, Baghdad, the old bazaar,
head swivelling, fingers curled, roars

from behind, the dry, red dirt ablaze.
The flattening, scorching chopper blades.

His trolley rolling slowly to a halt
where silver hammers hang

in gleaming rows. His sobs.
The shop till's momentary pause.

Team Photo

(Hindu Kush, Afghanistan, 1992)

After the Taliban,
under a barrel in the village square,
six amputated hands.

I played football there once.
Posed, afterwards, thumbs up.
Peace upon us as our jeep moved on.

I find the picture, curled in an attic box,
study its jury of faces one-by-one:
shy, wary, ebullient.

Who now dresses with one arm?
Who held whom in place
as the blade came down?

Tauromachy

(Guggenheim Venice, September 2019)

Tauromachy, it's called, this sculpture.
A severed bull's head, bronze, wedged
into the earth inches from its master's feet.
He – an abstracted pot-bellied farmer

with rod legs and a staff for a head –
is steering his invisible herd along
an ancient track, dogs busy at the rear,
silent amidst the bellowing.

I look over to where you are leaning into
the line of a Giacometti and think to tell you,
later, how I'm back to the first time I met
your father. Watching him *hoosh* the last

of the cattle through a gap in a ditch
as we approached. How he sucked the pith
from a cigarette as he sized me up.
The tossed butt sizzling in a puddle.

The way you squeezed my hand and said
you're in as he receded into the hollow
of the top field like a matador
departing, undefeated, from the ring.

WEST

You took me further west, out past Belmullet,
under a sky of milk and pewter
and blue eggs
in the rusting Mitsubishi Colt
you dubbed the Silver Bullet.

A day's gallivanting
led us to an off-road inlet,
seaweed marmalading the black shore,
the panel-beaten sea
cresting like blown-free bunting.

You clowned about in rocks,
your parka two sizes too big,
your hands swallowed by its sleeves,
the lightning strips of your legs
earthed in black docs.

I took a photo of you loose
and skittish under a bare hawthorn,
eyes crossed, tongue hanging sideways,
your head lassoed
by the hood's furry noose.

On the beach near where we stayed,
I fell over attempting a headstand,
surfaced dizzy in the storm-soar
of your laugh, lay on you, eyes closed
as the light began to fade.

You took me further west
to where I had not been before,
to where I fell down-ways,
side-ways, headlong
into your hidden, thumping nest.

HEM

Evenings when
you were not yet back
I'd sit on the makeshift
bench in the yard

of our first house
where you'd hung
a line with room
for just one dress

and close my eyes
and wait for the breeze
to lift your hem
against my knees.

Limbo

The ward reduces to its midnight hush.
A week since you were born six weeks too soon,

we keep vigil in this touch-less limbo.
Your face a miniature in distance,

your fingers gripping invisible lines.
Deirdre expressing to your silent cries.

In the small hours, without a word, a nurse
releases you into your mother's arms.

Sensing your breath in that titanic hold,
I wrap my shaking self around you both.

ARK

Rain – jungle rain, Niagaran rain,
end-of-days rain – hammering the roof
and you not home, 2am, your mother
worrying – *still no sign of him* –
and me in bed beside her smiling
at the thought of you freewheeling past
the Met Office – rain shooting off
its cupped satellite dishes –
down Washerwoman's Hill, no hands,
your wheels throwing up water-ski arcs of spray,
speeding up as you near the bridge,
your spokes spinning like turbines,
your glowing face lifted to the deluge,
your hair streaming like a comet's tail
as you take to the air, clear the bulwark
and land, sliding, on the deck of the Ark,
giraffes and ocelots scattering,
the scent of cedar unloosed where you stop
feet from Noah who shakes his head
from under a yellow sou-wester
as he turns the prow for Drumcondra,
and beyond, for Ararat,
the sky brightening to the east
as you leap into the garden
the rain easing and your mother
slipping into the deepest of sleeps.

THE SICKBED OF SHANE MCGOWAN

Backyard, Mulligans, Kilburn High.
Broken glass shapes out the constellations –
the Plough toppled sideways in its tracks,
the Hunter banging his jammed gun,
the Great Bear slumped against an outhouse jakes.

Earlier, inside, for your encore,
you held up a baton - your middle finger:
at its command, your boys jumped down
demented from the stage, smashing –
against the walls, against the floors,
against the thick skulls of the past –
their instruments' burnished wood.

Now, a tossed glass from the lock
you once forced open, the city's pent-up
foul spills through your sluice-gate –
down broken pipes, down sewers, down dreams,
into a tune already written.

STARTING OVER

The witching hour when sleep rises up
but stops below our bank and you lie
there exposed to what was hidden by the day.
Night twitches, polyps with intent,

as I walk the dog on wet streets, stare up
at top floor windows for sudden silhouettes,
wondering what torments are swirling
beneath duvets and tossed sheets.

Men in half-lit cubes click and scroll,
enlarge, delete, grow old. A child climbs
into his mother's bed. Skinny girls
adjust their camera-phones.

A fox walks down the centre of the road
looking for a dream to enter.
A police car slows behind, slaps on its siren,
disports itself further into the chasm.

The dog cocks his leg. I light a cigarette knowing
you are lighting a cigarette and dawn will soon
seep through, your hair brushing my face,
our breath bobbing, adrift on the same mild swell.

Acknowledgements

I owe a huge debt of gratitude to Tom French for his wise mentorship and unsparing fidelity to the art of poetry. A huge thanks also to Vicky Morris, sage poetic counsellor and fellow traveller; to Iggy McGovern, Colette Bryce, John McAuliffe, John O'Donnell and Jude Nutter, who have given of themselves so generously along the way; to Fergus Cronin for the sharing and encouragement.

There are so many others to thank: Martin Walsh for the Laneway Readings and everything else; Paul Rouse for the constructive insights; Greg Prendergast for the literary companionship; Paul Murphy for his camaraderie and support; my friends in Goatstown, Glasnevin, Kerry and in the world of law.

I would not be the person I am without the love, passion and sense of justice of my parents, Nollaig and Vera, and my soulmate siblings Diarmaid, Tríona and Muireann.

A special thanks to my wonderful children, Luan and Síofra, who inspire me and teach me every day.

Most of all, to Deirdre, to whom this book is dedicated – up to the moon.

Many thanks to the editors of the following publications in which a number of the poems in this collection appeared:

Atrium – 'West' and 'Limbo'

Crannóg – 'Hem' and 'Garden Shed'

Cyphers – 'Ghost Ship'

Poetry Wales – 'Last Tour' and 'Team Photo'

Prole – 'The Sickbed of Shane McGowan'

Southword – 'Last Rites'

The Honest Ulsterman – 'Ark'

The Lonely Crowd – 'My Uncle the Recluse' and 'Starting Over'

'Garden Shed' was anthologised in *Local Wonders: poems of our immediate surrounds* (ed. Pat Boran, Dedalus Press, 2021)

'Snowball' won the 2019 Westival International Poetry Competition

'Last Rites' was a runner-up in the 2020 Gregory O'Donoghue International Poetry Competition

'Keeper' was commended in the 2021 Troubadour International Poetry Competition

Printed in Great Britain
by Amazon

82464934R10021